D0841108

Victor Not Victim

My Battle with Hodgkin's Lymphoma

Dr. Mark Gugliotti, PT

iUniverse, Inc.
New York   Bloomington

Victor Not Victim
My Battle with Hodgkin's Lymphoma

iUniverse books may be ordered through booksellers or by contacting:

iUniverse
1663 Liberty Drive
Bloomington, IN 47403
www.iuniverse.com
1-800-Authors (1-800-288-4677)

ISBN: 978-1-4401-3452-4 (pbk)
ISBN: 978-1-4401-3453-1 (ebk)

Printed in the United States of America

iUniverse rev. date: 4/23/2009

To my friends in Port Jefferson.
Stay well and I promise to
do the same. ☮ ♡ ☺
Mark

To the countless individuals who walked with me throughout my journey back to health but, especially, my beloved wife, Irma, who carried me much of the way.

Special thanks to my cousin, Lynn, who God has truly blessed.

Contents

Introduction

AS A PHYSICAL THERAPIST, I'm constantly meeting new patients seeking my services to help them recover from whatever ails them. Over the years, I've learned many skills that have aided me greatly, but none as important as listening. Patients will often come to the office with a litany of concerns and quandaries, hoping someone might finally listen to them.

That's where I come in.

Initially, I largely help them understand the complex things happening inside their bodies. After that, we develop a game plan that will help them get back to their normal routines.

Not too long ago, I had the good fortune of being diagnosed with cancer. I know that sounds rather absurd, but it's true. As I underwent the barrage of tests and treatments, I had the pleasure of meeting many others just like me. I found myself intrigued with each person's story of how he or she was getting through the cancer. And while each person's experience was unique, I couldn't help but notice that there was a lot of overlap. In many cases, his or her needs were very similar in nature to those of my own patients, so I felt right at home. This was the good fortune part.

As I listened to them, I found I was able to share my own personal experiences and offer them advice that many found both helpful and comforting. These casual conversations would happen in waiting rooms, treatment areas, and even locker rooms, where the only thing between me and my neighbor was our thin cotton gowns.

The following pages are an attempt to share my cancer story with you in the same way I did with so many of the other patients I had the pleasure of meeting along the way. Unfortunately, some of them will never have the opportunity to read it, but I hope they're somewhere, still laughing about the goofy things I shared with them.

I also included the e-mails I sent throughout my ordeal. They are inserted at the end of the appropriate chapters. The pictures attached to some of them were taken the day of my treatment. While it's easy to see the physical toll from treatment to treatment, please take note that the one thing that never changed was my smile.

Chapter One:
I Have a *What* in My Chest?

ALL RIGHT. WELL, NOW that I think about it, I find it pretty ironic that, one year later after the first cough, I have another one, but know it's not for the same reason. About February of 2007 was when it really began to get to a point where I wanted to start checking into it.

Until then I had this dry, nonproductive cough. Apparently, it had been going on before then, but I just never realized it. I had just chalked it up to a winter cold and some postnasal drip, but my wife and others around me had already begun to take notice. In fact, my wife probably noticed it more because it started to keep us both up at night.

I should mention that I was also jogging for exercise at the time. After a cold weather run, my windpipe would suddenly close after I came inside. Although short-lived, this made it a bit tough to take a full breath, and it often sparked a coughing frenzy. This recurrent experience led me to believe I had a touch of exercise-induced asthma.

Sounds reasonable, doesn't it? It's not so uncommon, and it certainly would fit the picture. At that point, I decided to have a doctor check it out.

I probably should also mention a little bit about my own health history. Whenever I caught a cold, whether nasal or chest, it always seemed to stay with me much longer than most people. We're talking weeks to a month or so. Coincidence or not, that's just how it was.

So, getting back to the doctor.

I made the appointment. Of course, like usual, I was feeling fine and had no cough. I didn't have a single symptom to offer that might indicate an infection. The doctor and I engaged in a little Q&A, and then he performed a routine physical exam.

My doctor is really great. He's a nice guy, and he's also very knowledgeable. At the end of the examination, he said I should see how it goes and go for a pulmonary function test (PFT) in the meantime. This certainly made the most sense, and working for a hospital would make this even easier. All I had to do was call the pulmonary department and schedule a time to check my breathing.

I was able to be tested a few days after my doctor's visit and yup, you guessed it, my cough had come back. It was just as dry, hacking, and nonproductive as ever. So I went to the pulmonary department, where I was greeted by a respiratory therapist who explained exactly what the test was and how I was to do it.

Using a mouthpiece, I had to breathe into a machine that would then tell us how well my lungs were actually doing. For each test, I couldn't help but cough throughout because that was all I seemed to be doing lately. The therapist reassured me I was doing fine and said the preliminary findings looked good.

I thought, "How can it look good when I've just about hacked up a lung at this point?" The therapist said, "Go home and try to take it easy. The results should be back in a couple of days."

When they did, I was very surprised to find my lung function was pretty much normal, except for diminished residual volume. It also said that an external compression source, such as obesity, should be considered.

I actually found it somewhat comical. Of course, the pulmonologist who read the PFT didn't know me from Adam except for what he had read on paper. At five-foot-four and one hundred fifty-eight pounds, this wasn't quite the answer I had hoped for, so I thought I'd just see how it went for a while. Even though it did show something, I was sure it was really nothing to worry about. After all, it was just a cough.

Two months passed. It was April, and I was still coughing. I was really tired of my cough and so has everyone else including my wife who was just about ready to kick me out of bed. Thank God for the spare bedroom! Otherwise I would certainly be couch bound downstairs. In May, I finally decided to see a pulmonologist.

In addition to the cough, I had also developed an insanely aggravating itch that seemed to pop up out of nowhere. Whenever I scratched the itchy patches, the skin became raised and inflamed, but then subsided within five minutes. This had only started happening over the past month. I had thought to go to an allergist, thinking that a cough plus itching equaled an allergy. It was an unusually high allergy season with many people suffering that normally wouldn't. I thought I could be one of them.

So we changed dryer sheets, detergents, soaps, and shampoo. Nothing seemed to help, and we even considered our dog, Molly. It would have killed me to get rid of her, but it didn't seem to matter. By now, my coughing had gotten even worse.

So, back to finding a pulmonologist.

Patients of mine had highly recommended a pulmonary practice just down the street from where I worked and I was happy to find they accepted my insurance. Knowing they accepted my insurance along with the recommendations and my level of frustration helped to make the choice of this practice an easy one. Again, it was just a cough.

When I finally contacted the doctor's office, I was told I needed to have a recent chest x-ray for him to view. I was able to have the chest film taken at the hospital where I work and I was now ready to meet the man who would tell me I had some weird thing that needed two weeks of antibiotics to clear. Then I could continue with a cough-free life.

When I got to the office, I was pleasantly greeted and asked to fill out a bit of paperwork. After taking a discreet look around the room, I couldn't help notice that I was, by far, the youngest person in the office. It was almost as if I had to do a mental check to see if I really needed to be here. Then I coughed. It really wasn't troublesome. After all, I'm in health care. I know anyone can have a problem, no matter how young or old one is. It's just strange when it's you.

The doctor came out and led me to his office, where I brought him up to speed with the situation. He asked about the progression of things and wanted to know how I was doing now. The doctor also looked at the x-ray and read the report that stated normal findings for both views. We continued to discuss my family's history with asthma, chronic bronchitis, lung cancer and a few others. But my problem was just a cough, remember?

After our discussion he brought me into his examination room and gave me a thorough once-over from head to chest. Satisfied with his examination, he mentioned that he'd like to have two more things to help reach a diagnosis: a repeat of the PFT in his office (to compare the values from the previous test) and a CAT scan of my chest. Being satisfied with his recommendations, I left to schedule both appointments. The strangest feeling came over me at that very same moment.

I turned to the doctor and said, "I know that you're the one who's going to find out what's going on with me."

He smiled and headed back to his office.

The following week, I came back to his office to repeat the PFT. It was the same as before. I coughed a lot. The CAT scan was a whole other animal. Of course, I chose to have my scan at the hospital where I work. After checking in, I was led to the room with the machine. I was asked to lie down on the machine's sliding bed. The machine looked like a squared-off breath mint. The small bed slides you through the center hole.

Once the physician assistant injected me with the contrast dye, to which I have no allergy; I was gradually slid into the hole while being asked to breathe in and out. After each part of my chest was scanned, I was free to go. There wasn't even the slightest discomfort or unpleasantry throughout the entire procedure.

Finally, one week later, the day for my follow-up appointment with the pulmonologist arrived. You can only imagine my excitement in being one step closer to ridding myself of this annoying cough. He would probably say that I should use something as simple as an inhaler taken as needed with a little something for the itching.

I drove over to the office. The doctor then asked me to follow him into his office. After closing his door he sat down and started gathering reports from my file.

He asked, "How are you doing?"

"Fine," I said.

He said, "I've found what is causing you to cough so much. You have a tumor growing inside your chest, and it's pressing up against your windpipe, causing you to cough."

Nothing could ever have been such a more distant thought in my mind than a tumor.

Stunned, I responded, "I have a *what* in my chest?"

He said, "A tumor."

I sat back, falling deeper in my chair.

In a more somber tone, I said, "Really?"

Of all the things I suppose I could have been at that precise moment in my life, I intuitively fell back on the old reliable and became the typical, inquisitive me. It was my classic coping strategy of "What is it?" and "How do I get rid of it?"

I asked, "What do you think it is?"

He said, "It's pretty hard to tell for sure until it is biopsied."

The doctor said he had already taken the liberty of making an appointment with a surgeon he wanted me to see, but it was up to me to follow his recommendation.

Now, even though the tumor thing was still sort of settling in, I said, "You've got to be kidding me if you think I'm going in a different direction than the one you're suggesting."

My doctor was a real grab the bull by the horns sort of guy and I had come to trust him implicitly without question. His professionalism and genuine concern for my well- being was nothing short of praiseworthy.

After some respectfully desperate probing on my part, he offered a few possible tumor types that could be the guilty party, but a biopsy would obviously be the next necessary step in the process.

Everything he had mentioned was treatable. Of course, some had a better prognosis than others did.

At the end of our discussion, the doctor said, "I want to see you for a follow-up appointment in a couple months. In the meantime, let me know if you have any problems that I can help you with." He then paused, and asked, "What are you planning on doing for the rest of the afternoon?"

I answered, "I'm going to get some pizza 'cause I'm freakin' starving right now!"

He smiled. I thanked him again and then headed out of the office.

Now, for most people, I think that would seem like the difficult part, but not so. The next hour was the really hard part. These were the first moments in time where I was completely by myself, and I definitely felt it. I also had to go home and report everything to my wife. Telling her I had cancer was going to be one of the most difficult things I ever had to do. I still really wasn't able to say, what for a short while became known as the other *C*-word. I felt a little more comfortable calling it a tumor. I know that seems kind of strange, but cancer carried so much doom and gloom with it that I just wasn't comfortable with all that baggage yet.

I drove to the pizza place and went inside to place the order. I then sat on a bench, feeling dumbfounded. I started to fill up inside, wondering if I'd make it another six months to celebrate Christmas.

I thought, "Am I going to see any of the new construction projects I drive by every day finished before I die? Am I really going to die?"

Yeah, I was starting to do a number on myself. By now, family after family was starting to walk by me while heading for the pizza buffet. There I sat with tears streaming down my face and my chin trembling. What got to me the most was that Irma and I had started our adoption process about a year ago. Of course, I couldn't help but think that we would never be a family. A new all-time low had reached the pit of my stomach. Just a few months ago, I had turned to my wife during a morning walk and told her how blessed I was to have my life so complete at such a young age.

The pizza seemed to be taking forever, and all I wanted to do was leave.

I asked one of the servers, "Could I just have a single piece of pizza from the buffet, to comfort me while I waited?"

She answered, "No, it's only for those who paid!"

Desperate, I said, "Just a slice. I could really use a slice right now."

She had no clue, but no meant no. Feeling defeated, I just sat there and waited for my order. I finally got the order and headed out to my car, still holding in a waterfall of tears.

The drive back home was about fifteen minutes. Then I'd have to tell Irma that I had a tumor in my chest. Throughout the drive, I just kept going over how I would tell her everything I had to. As I drove by many works-in-project, I again wondered if I was going to make it long enough to see them completed.

At that point I lost it and starting sobbing.

As I pulled up to the house, I thought I would wait for just the right moment, but I realized there was no right moment to tell the most important person in your life something like this. I walked inside while looking for the moment. Irma was in the kitchen, cleaning things up and making the house look nice, just like she always does. I tried to make it seem like nothing was wrong, but I couldn't even convince myself of that.

Irma and I both exchanged a kiss and a smile.

"Hello," I said.

She asked, "How's the day going?"

I said, "Okay."

She said, "The pizza smells pretty good."

I said, "Yeah, we should eat it while it's warm."

I moved around the kitchen, looking for the right spot to start the whole delivery. I first sat in a chair and then stood near a door, but I couldn't get it going. Finally, for the first time, a man never short of words was quiet. I started to move closer to Irma. I helped her get the silverware out from the drawer.

She asked, "So how did you make out at the doctor's?"

I froze and tried to say, "I have a tumor."

But nothing came out, even though my mouth was moving. There was no sound, even though I heard myself saying it inside. I finally got it out.

"It's not good," I said. "I have a tumor growing inside my chest."

I still wasn't sure if she heard it.

Irma asked, "What?"

But her question wasn't in disbelief.

I said, "I have a tumor."

She immediately started crying as she hugged me.

9

Repeatedly, she said, "Oh, no, Marky. I'm so sorry."

I just said to her, "Don't worry it's going to be all right."

I don't know how I could say that but I felt I had to console her in some way. We slowly started to make our way to the table while still sobbing and hugging each other, trying to get a handle on this.

Once we were sitting, I said, "Now let me explain what the doctor said to me."

I told her the whole story, just as he had laid it out for me.

"I have a tumor about two centimeters by three centimeters by five centimeters. It's pressing up against my windpipe, but he wasn't really sure what it was. I gotta go for a biopsy."

I had to go and do all those things we hear about from our patients but never really think we're going to have to do. We sat and cried. While sitting, I realized how much I was shaking inside. Maybe it was the whole tumor thing. Maybe it was because I hadn't eaten lunch yet. Anyway, I suggested we eat something. I must say the pizza never tasted better than it did that day. At this point, we were just trying to let it all sink in. That was that.

The next person I was going to have to tell wasn't going to be any easier. I had to call my parents, and, of course, Irma had to call hers. So I called my mom. I wasn't really saying anything about the doctor's visit just yet.

She asked, "Well, did you get the results?"

I said, "Yeah."

She said, "Well?"

I said, "Well, they're not good. There seems to be a tumor inside my chest."

She said, "Oh, Mark."

In these past few weeks, my mother had found out that her daughter-in-law had breast cancer and her own mother's health was failing. She really didn't know what to say at that point, so I tried to console her by further explaining the details of everything. After we spoke about all the things I would need to do I said, "I'll tell Dad myself."

And I did when he got home from work. Of course, to follow would be a similar conversation with my brother and Irma's family.

I think Irma had it a little tougher. Not only did she have to translate everything into Dutch, but she had to do it while she was still digesting everything. It wasn't an easy situation by any means, but we all agreed to do the best we could until the biopsy and then go from there. We also agreed to hold off until then before we alerted the masses. Otherwise, it would have turned into one huge game of telephone and that wouldn't have been helpful for anyone.

Driving to work the next day and telling my staff wasn't too easy either. Alone in the car, I would just start crying. Thankfully, that only lasted a few days. I just had to focus on the here and now while I waited for the biopsy.

June 24 (Letter to Irma's Brother and Sister-In-Law Regarding Tumor)

Well, Well Family,

It would appear both Irma and I are in for an interesting ride. After all, who would have imagined that anything like this could happen? One thing is for certain, your support is appreciated and comforting. At this point Irma and I are looking at things rather realistically and both feel more positively than anything else. For now we will take each day one at a time. We've always been good at this and together we'll continue to be there for each other. Although there is a bit of distance between us, I can assure you that your love and prayers keep you close to my heart.

We promise to keep you updated. Please kiss the boys for us and thanks for the picture.

With much health and love,

Mark and Irma

Chapter Two:
SO WHAT ARE YOU IN FOR?

LET'S HAVE A RECAP. A simple dry cough and some itchy skin eventually led me to a pulmonologist, who subsequently sent me for a CAT scan of my chest. Uh-oh, there was a tumor in the chest. Next step was biopsy.

I'd still go back and read Chapter One for the fillers if you haven't done so already.

Exactly one week after the tumor news I had my surgical consult with the surgeon. I was so very happy to have Irma going with me to this visit, for both comfort and support. I had a feeling that, from this point on, things were going to move along pretty quickly for the both of us.

We headed into the office and got squared away with the paperwork. Both Irma and I had noticed the doctor was also Chief of Thoracic Surgery. So far, throughout this whole ordeal, I couldn't help but notice a feeling of being led along the way. This was just one of many instances that I'd take note of.

Not much longer after that, we were brought to an examination room where a general history and vitals (height, weight, and so forth) were taken. Then we waited a few more minutes for the surgeon. When he walked in and introduced himself, I felt immediately relieved because it was easy to see what a kind and caring man he was.

We had briefly overheard him in the hallway while he was having a phone conversation with his mom. By his manner, we could almost imagine that she was just calling to see how his day was going.

We were soon talking in greater detail about the two possible biopsy procedures needed. The less invasive of the two would require a same-day procedure in which a small incision would be made just above the collarbone, allowing access to the tumor for a biopsy. The more invasive would require an overnight stay, two small incisions between ribs along my left side, deflation of my left lung for easier tumor access, biopsy, and re-inflation of the lung.

Yup! You guessed it. I was having lucky number two.

Now, of course, there was a good reason for it. If they went with the first option and found they couldn't get to the tumor so easily, they would have to stop everything and prep me for the second option anyway. Suddenly, the second option clearly became the better choice.

Of course, I asked, "So what do you think it could be?"

He said exactly what the pulmonologist had said, "We'll have to wait for the biopsy."

At least everyone was on the same payroll.

I was told to schedule an appointment for pre-surgical testing to make sure I was healthy enough for the surgery. I would also be given instructions about getting ready for the surgery, for example, eating, drinking, showering, and so forth. My appointment was just before

Independence Day. I had to go to the hospital's pre-surgical testing department. Again, similar to the other office visits, I was the youngest one there.

After waiting a little while, a woman sat down across from me. We smiled at each other. A few seconds later I leaned forward, smiled, and asked, "So what are you in for?"

She smiled, laughed and then said, "Oh, just another cancer surgery."

She had been battling colon cancer for some time and seemed to be making progress. When she had finished explaining a few more of the details regarding her cancer, I said, "I'm sure that everything will be alright."

She smiled and said, "I agree."

As we continued to share our tales, it became clear to me that she was truly a woman of faith. Little by little, we started talking more about our shared spiritual beliefs, how things just seem to always work out, or how often we were referred to as being lucky all the time.

We laughed and chatted about how important our faith was. We felt blessed to notice the wonderful gifts God gives to us every day, like meeting each other. It made us both feel special inside. That same feeling helped me feel at peace. I knew I was never really alone.

This lovely woman knew exactly what I was talking about, and she said she felt exactly the same way. And that's why everything was really going to be all right for both of us. We saw each of our ordeals as a cross to bear, but we knew that we wouldn't be bearing them alone. All we needed to do was ask and pray for the strength to do so. With this strength, I could take a more active (rather than passive) roll in my care.

She said that it was important to keep doing things she was used to doing, despite any pitfalls along the way. At this moment, I realized I would commit myself to the same outlook and tackle anything that came my way. Just a few minutes later, I was called in, but, before I left, the woman and I hugged. We both said we would pray for each other.

Once inside the room, the nurse took all my vitals and a little bit of blood. She explained where I'd be going on biopsy day and said I'd have to fast before the surgery. She also gave me antibacterial scrubbing sponges for when I showered on the morning of the biopsy to make me extra clean. She said I couldn't wear any jewelry. I wasn't too happy about that because I had only taken off my wedding band once in my seven years of marriage.

"Do you have any questions?" she asked.

I said, "No."

The nurse wished me well, and I went home. The biopsy was scheduled for July 10, just two days after my birthday. Despite everything that was going on, I was determined to make my thirty-seventh year of life a positive and productive one.

My parents had come down the night before the biopsy so they could go with us to the hospital. So, while they enjoyed breakfast, I was scrubbing down in the shower and getting ready to go. Irma had gotten me a couple of beautiful cards and a bag of very sentimental charms, which I put in my overnight bag. Before we left, I also got a call from my in-laws, who were wishing me well. We drove to the hospital, and off to pre-op I went.

I was given a fashionable gown to change into and I removed all metal.

I asked Irma, "Can you take my ring from me? I expect it back." I gave her a hug and a kiss while saying, "I love you."

Let's not forget the parents. It was the same for them, too.

We walked down the hall until only the transporter and I could go on. I gave another quick kiss to Irma before we both said, "I'll see you later."

I was wheeled down the hall and parked just outside the operating room. It looked like some kind of science-fiction movie was going to be filmed inside. There were video towers and computers as well as all the other shiny things that you'd expect to see in an operating room.

I had a few moments so I asked God to help my surgeon and the other staff members to bring their A-game today and just help me through this next step.

About five seconds later, my surgeon walked around the corner and asked, "How is it going?"

I said, "Really well. I'm ready when you are."

We told each other a couple of jokes.

I asked, "Can I watch?"

He reminded me of why that might be a bad idea. A sharp object in the chest of a patient who was awake and might cough was never a good thing. I trusted his judgment and settled for a picture instead.

With that, I was wheeled in, transferred to the table of honor, given a slight sedative, and asked to count back from ten. I think I got to seven.

The next thing I remember, I was waking up in post-op, feeling a bit out of it and coughing uncontrollably. I was trying to figure out what the hell was happening.

Everyone was asking how I was doing. I said I was thirsty and wanted something to drink. I was able to strike a bargain with ice chips, which I just let melt in my mouth and turn to water anyhow. At least my brain still seemed intact.

I was also having a tough time breathing, but, I was told it would get easier when my lung was fully reinflated. I was given a small device to practice my breathing with.

I saw my surgeon a minute or two after. He let me know everything went well. He pointed out the small drain that would eventually be removed along the side of my ribs.

I asked, "What do you think the tumor was most likely to be?"

He answered, "It looks like Hodgkin's lymphoma, but we'll have to wait until the pathology lab could confirm that."

I immediately asked, "Did you tell my family yet? Can I see them?"

He replied, "Yes. You can see them soon."

I said, "Thanks for everything."

He smiled and said, "You're welcome."

Incidentally, he did show me a picture of the inside of my chest and it looked pretty cool. So now I knew I had cancer, but I still had to wait and see what kind.

Irma and my mother were both allowed to come in for a short visit.

They asked, "So, how are you doing?"

I said, "Pretty okay, but really thirsty, and now even hungry. The doctor said that it looked like Hodgkin's disease, but we need to wait for the report."

They both said, "He has already discussed everything with us."

Weeks later, both my mother and Irma told me that after the procedure, he had come out to see them. But, instead of telling them in the waiting area, like many of the other surgeons, he asked them to come into a private room.

Irma kept asking herself, "Why can't he just tell us here? Why do we have to go into a private room?"

Of course, deep down inside she knew the real answer.

After hearing him mention the likelihood of Hodgkin's, they were devastated to say the least, but they also noticed the angst and disappointment in his eyes as well. I took comfort in the old adage "strength in numbers" because I could only imagine what it must be like to be alone and have to hear news of that nature. I also realized how difficult it must have been for the surgeon. That morning we were all gunning for any and all things noncancerous, but that wasn't to be the case that day. The best thing we could do now was just wait for the results and focus on the post-op recovery.

At this point, I was enjoying the ice chip melting even more. I realized that taking slower breaths was a little easier. I had been in recovery long enough to start the transfer upstairs.

A nurse asked, "Can I get you anything before you leave?"

I said, "Do you think they could send me up a turkey sandwich or something. I'm starving!"

My grandfather used to always say, "You need fire in the furnace to keep it going."

She smiled and said, "I'll work on it."

I was wheeled upstairs and finally taken into my room where, lo and behold, sat a food tray with a turkey sandwich, Jell-O, and cranberry juice. It was the most delicious turkey sandwich I had ever eaten!

It was a shared room, but my neighbor's curtain was drawn for privacy. Irma and my parents arrived shortly after my feast. The nurse had also come in to check on me and let me know I could use the bathroom as long as I felt comfortable enough. I just needed to pee into a container so my output could be measured. That would actually be my ticket out of there. As long as I was without fever and kept up on my fluids and energy levels, I could possibly make it home that night. I immediately set my sights on an early departure and began drinking any and all fluids within my reach.

Now, don't get me wrong! I was a little uncomfortable moving around, but I still had the good drugs inside of me from the surgery. I kept up with my breathing exercises, and I was able to get the little ball up to the top of the chamber, though not each time.

I began taking little walking trips around the floor with my IV pole, and I eventually turned them into laps. It really was just like walking around a track except no lines on the floor and no runners in the fast lane. First my dad walked with me, then Irma, and I even managed a few on my own. I always wondered if the nurses had a secret pool going to see if I'd make it out that night or not. Regardless, they were great.

It was finally getting close to dinner. I realized I had been in the room for about five hours when my surgeon's assistant stopped in to see how I was doing. I had been drinking, snacking, breathing, walking and peeing as much as I could. He was really pleased to find me doing so well. He said that I could probably go home that night. He just needed to double-check with the surgeon. About another hour later, I got the news I was looking for. I was going home!

The physician assistant came in shortly after and gave me the once-over. He checked the drain, removed it, and put in a couple of stitches to close the wound. Although this was a little uncomfortable, I was going home, so who really cared?

We went over washing procedures to protect the surgical site. I was asked to keep an eye out for any fever.

I said, "Thank you."

The physician assistant said, "You're welcome."

I was given two prescriptions to fill and my street clothes to change into. My mom stayed with me while I was transported by wheelchair to the pick up area. Irma and my dad were waiting with the truck. And home we went. As we got closer to home, we quickly stopped at the local pharmacy to fill my prescriptions.

It was good to be home! We let our dog, Molly, out. She was very eager to visit her favorite little tree across the street. It was relaxing to be at home and still have that sense of calmness and peace despite the not-so-good news. All we had to do was wait it out until the pathology report came back.

The next couple weeks kept us somewhat busy. We seemed to be hit from every direction. Just two days following my biopsy, my grandmother passed away due to complications from stomach cancer. Her health had begun a slow decline over the past couple of months. Thankfully, my sister-in-law who was managing with her breast cancer was overcoming the obstacles that faced her. She eventually went on to beat it.

As for me, I was just trying to take it easy and keep my lung and spirits inflated. At first I would use the pain medication to help take the edge off sleeping, but I had stopped after four days. The scar was healing well, and the stitches weren't even really a factor. They would dissolve on their own over time, so I just tried not to let them catch on my clothes.

I had taken off a few days from work and returned the following week. It felt good to stay in the game while also breathing more easily with each passing day. On the Monday just before the follow-up appointment, now two weeks after the biopsy, I made the first of two poor choices throughout my whole ordeal.

21

Feeling as well as I did, I decided to return to the gym. I knew enough to not lift any heavy weights or push myself as I normally would, but I wanted to try something. After doing a little bit of stretching and some biceps curls, I figured I'd try my hand at some assisted pull-ups. Using the machine's platform and its counterweight, I felt it would allow me a safe transition back to a regular workout routine. I kept my reps to ten and only did that twice with a feeling of accomplishment and no added discomfort. When I got back home, I told Irma how well it went. Of course, this made her just as happy.

About four hours after we went to bed, I woke up in more pain than I had after the surgery. It was pretty hard to breathe. The only position that granted me any relief was kneeling down and bending forward, similar to the child pose in yoga. It was evident that just the little I had done at the gym was way too much for now. All the little muscles between my ribs where they cut me were awake and throwing a little party.

All that easy recovery breathing came to a screeching halt that evening. Irma, bless her heart, did everything she could to make her fool husband as comfortable as she could. Never once did she say, "I told you so" or "You're an idiot," unlike some of you right now.

I managed to sleep that night, but I would still experience a similar discomfort during the next couple of weeks. Two days following that poor choice, we went for the scheduled follow-up appointment. It was somewhat funny when the physician assistant asked me if I was starting to walk longer distances since the surgery.

When I told her what I had been doing she shook her head and looked at my wife as if to say, "Is he for real?" We didn't say much more than that, and then the surgeon came in.

He asked, "How is everything going."

I said, "Everything is going okay except for a little workout mishap, but I'm on the mend."

At this point, I just couldn't help but ask about the pathology results. My doctor said the pathology lab had confirmed his suspicion of Hodgkin's lymphoma. He said I would need to undergo further testing under the care of an oncologist to help stage the cancer. This would help determine how progressed it was and which treatments I would receive.

It was the kind of news we somewhat expected but we still weren't too thrilled to hear, though, by now, we knew that the prognosis of Hodgkin's lymphoma was pretty good. At this point, it was really important to keep things in perspective.

The surgeon said, "You'll need to undergo some additional testing for the staging."

I asked, "Will they have to do a brain scan?"

He smiled and said, "Probably not. They wouldn't find anything up there anyway."

He really was a great guy. The doctor made some suggestions for consultations and made it clear that we could call him whenever we needed to. Irma and I both thanked the surgeon for all he had done for us and went out into the parking lot to call our families with the news.

I also reached out to a doctor friend who worked at Memorial Sloan-Kettering Cancer Center for direction. His assistance in this matter would prove invaluable.

July 25 (Letter to Friends and Family Regarding Biopsy Results)

Hello My Friends,

I figured I'd bring all of you up to speed at the same time to make things a little bit easier to keep track of. If I hadn't spoken to you prior to this e-mail it doesn't mean that I think you dress funny or say silly things (cause God knows I've cornered the market on that).

By now, some of you are aware of a recent biopsy that was necessary to determine what the little tumor growing inside my chest was made of (and it wasn't a snake, snail or a puppy dog tail). The labs came back to confirm Hodgkin's Disease. For those of you who might be unfamiliar with this, it's simply a cancer of the lymph nodes and lymph system in our bodies. This system is responsible for the removal of larger waste products from the blood stream. Sounds bad, I know, but there is a light at the end of the tunnel. Hodgkin's lymphoma has a very high cure rate which I hope has now enabled you to catch your breath again. Of course, with everything there is still a catch. We have to first determine what Stage of the disease I'm in. The Stages range from 1-4.

Stage 1 being the best and Stage 4 being the not so best. I'm also seeing an oncologist in a couple of weeks who will put me through a few more testing procedures {lower abdominal CAT scan (easy), brain scan (easier because it's empty up there) PET scan (easy) and a bone marrow biopsy (not favoring a needle deep in my butt cheek)}. Once they know exactly where I stand, they can start getting me better.

So, you ask, how we're doing? We're doing well. Irma and I have been a tremendous strength for each other especially knowing how supportive you have been and will continue to be. My folks have been slapped around a bit too much over the last couple of weeks but it seems that they're on the mend.

This is certainly not something I'm keeping secret so if you happen to run into a mutual acquaintance (first apologize for running into him/ her) don't be afraid to share the news. I find that uncertainty only causes unnecessary concerns and worries. Besides, I have no secrets except for the ones I'm already holding a few of you to!

Oh yeah, I'm sending my new e-mail address to help us stay better connected.

> *Stay well and I'll promise to do the same,*
> *Mark*

Chapter Three:
THE C-WORD!

JUST TO AVOID ANY confusion, I have cancer. If you'd rather dress it up a little, it's Hodgkin's lymphoma. It took me a little while to say the C-word. It's always associated with such a bleak outlook that, at first, I felt more comfortable saying to people, "I have a tumor in my chest." But I knew I'd only get going in the right direction if I heard myself talking about it more freely. I even practiced saying, "I have cancer" in the mirror just for the reinforcement. After a couple of dry runs, I had it licked.

So now I had to find out what stage of the disease I was in. For that, I needed a little help. My friend who worked at Memorial Sloan-Kettering Cancer Center (MSK) immediately got back to me. He recommended one of his colleagues who could see me at the hospital's satellite clinic close by our home. Of course, the local satellite would be very convenient, but I was certainly willing to travel any distance necessary for the best care available and, more importantly, get the ball rolling.

When I called the local satellite, I found that, because of the sheer volume of patients being seen at the time, the soonest availability for consult would be about a month's time. I felt my stomach drop. I tried to remember if I had mentioned I had just been diagnosed with cancer, but realized, all of their patients were in the same boat. Yikes! It wasn't one of those things I felt I should blow-off.

I asked, "Are there any other possibilities?"

They said, "You could likely be seen at the Manhattan office pretty quickly and then transfer out to the satellite."

That made Irma and me feel a whole lot better inside. I immediately called the Manhattan office and made an appointment to be seen in two weeks. Although it was still two weeks away, it was a lot sooner than a month. Then, that little thing I spoke of earlier happened again. We got a call letting me know I could move my appointment up by a week because of a cancellation. There was still going to be a little trick to that. I had only had the CAT scan of the chest.

I still needed the other tests for the staging, plus MSK requires that the pathology slides of the biopsy be viewed by their pathology lab before any complete diagnosis was given. Now I was under the gun to get all these things done before my new appointment. Well, being a man on a mission, I set out to help it happen.

Getting the pathology slides to them was a snap. It just required a fee. But I still needed to sign up for the CAT scans of the abdomen and pelvis, the PET scan, and a bone marrow biopsy.

When I mentioned this, the office asked if I could come to the city a day earlier and have the CAT and PET scans done at a radiology clinic they often used. Because of its size and volume capacity, they would have no problem scheduling an appointment for me. Of course, I agreed.

The radiology clinic was able to see me on the day before my first oncology consult. The clinic was very helpful in setting up my scans and they were very clear on what I could eat and drink for the whole day before the testing. I was to avoid caffeine, nicotine, and alcohol. I also couldn't have anything to eat or drink other than water just before the testing. No problem, right?

That morning, I got up early enough to still have a little something in my stomach, but I took the dog for a longer walk than usual to help clear my mind. When I finally got back, Irma was pulling fresh rolls out of the oven. We put a little butter on our rolls and started eating. Just as I took a bite out of the other half of my roll, I noticed the time.

"Oh! My God! I'm not supposed to be eating!"

I was off by an hour, and I freaked out! We had both forgot. It was such a beautiful morning, and everything seemed just perfect. I ran upstairs to the bathroom and stuck my toothbrush as far back in my mouth as I could to try to make myself throw up. A little came up, but now I was just thinking of how much had made it into my system and if it would mess up any of the findings. After all, everything today had to be perfect. It was starting to get close to departure time so I brushed my teeth, rinsed, kissed Irma, and out the door I went.

Taking the train was the easiest option, so, once I got to the station and hopped on the train, I managed to calm myself down. Going in for the tests was actually a dry run for the doctor's visit the following day.

When I arrived, the secretary greeted me with yet more paperwork to fill out. I also noticed I was finally not the youngest patient in the office. I told them about the breakfast roll incidence and was relieved when they told me it wasn't a problem. After only a few minutes, I was called back and given a lovely blue gown. I wore nothing except underwear and socks underneath.

I was asked to drink a liter of the contrast liquid. Even though it was piña colada-flavored, please don't be misled into thinking that it was as tasty.

Now, for the special feature!

As I was still doing my best to gulp down this stuff, a nurse walked in with what looked to be a designer metal purse, but actually was a leaded case containing the radioactive sugar solution used for the PET scan. Once injected into my arm, it would travel for the next hour to all the areas of my body that used sugar for energy. The brain, heart, and a few other pieces of me, including the cancer, loves sugar. They would determine how active the cancer was by seeing how many sites showed a sugar uptake while comparing it to the findings of the CAT scan.

By now, I had started taking frequent trips to the little cowboy's room because of the fruity drink. During the last trip (and just moments before the actual testing), was when a very embarrassing thing happened. I had been told that I might experience a little diarrhea because of the barium drink, but didn't think anything of it because I really just needed to pee. However, during my moments standing above the bowl, I felt a little gas building up and I decided to let a little escape, but it wasn't just gas.

My recommendation to any man in a similar situation would be to sit down when peeing after finishing your barium cocktail. You could only imagine how I felt, especially because it was time for the scans. I could only quickly rinse out my shorts with soap and water and press the hand dryer button about twenty times until they were dry enough to not seep through the gown. Just to be on the safe side, because I knew I'd be lying on my back for a while, I decided to wear my boxers backwards.

The radiology technician met me outside the door, and he didn't appear suspicious at all. He led me into the scanning room, where a warm bed and blanket was waiting for me. The machine itself was the same kind used for my chest CAT scan except this one also did the PET scan. It certainly made things easier instead of having to change to another room. The tech took his time in explaining the testing procedure to make sure I understood everything. It turned out he did one of his early affiliations at the hospital I work for, so that was a little extra comfort bonus.

Once everything was set, I was slid through the opening. The CAT scanner started taking pictures of my belly and then my pelvis. Again, the only thing I really had to do was take deep breaths in and out while I kept my arms over my head. The machine did all the rest.

After the CAT scans were done, I was already in position for the PET scan to begin. This one lasted about forty minutes in total compared with the twenty-minute CAT scans. This was because it was scanning from my head to my knees. It also had to pick up the sugar signal, which was different than the barium cocktail.

I didn't mind at all. I had such an overwhelming sense of peace that I decided to pray a rosary. I wasn't allowed to move during the scan so I just gently pressed my finger tips against the blanket to help me keep count. I've always found that I feel better after praying, and it's easy enough to do. It also never hurts to ask for a little help from above.

Before I knew it, the PET scan was finished and I was saying, "Thank you" to everybody. I was told my results would be sent to the doctor's office well before my appointment tomorrow. Once I left, there was only one thing on my mind.

I thought, "Where is the closest fast-food joint?"

Thankfully, one was right in the train station, and the food tasted great!

On the train ride, I called Irma and my dad to let them know everything went well. I said that things should now go smoothly for the following day. Speaking of which, it was going to be a very early start. My appointment was at eleven o'clock in the morning which meant we needed to get up around five o'clock to get ready and catch an early train. And we did.

We made it without any delays and arrived about a half hour early. Of course, I had paperwork to do, but I had already downloaded most of it from MSK's Web site and filled it out. We didn't have to stay long in the waiting room before we were brought into an exam room, where we only waited about another five minutes for the oncologist.

He was a real down-to-earth guy who was about our age and very relaxing. He asked how we were doing and really listened to everything we said. We never once felt rushed. He talked about the biopsy findings and confirmed the diagnosis of Hodgkin's lymphoma.

Then he said, "Well, now for the scans."

It was if I heard a drum roll in the background.

He said, "They look pretty good."

Irma and I both smiled at each other, with a sigh of relief. The doctor explained that all the cancer was isolated to just my chest region and not my abdomen or pelvis. The PET scan showed all the little hot spots in my chest where the cancer was hanging out. At this point, the results were indicating Stage II lymphoma, but I still needed to have one more test to confirm that. The bone marrow biopsy was necessary to make sure nothing was growing in my bone marrow.

I had heard horror stories about how painful it was and how I should have someone drive me so I could lie down in the backseat on the ride home. So imagine my surprise when the doctor said, "If you'd like, I could do your bone marrow biopsy about an hour from now."

I looked at Irma with a little hesitation.

The doctor must have known what was going through my head. He said, "I've had sixty-year-old patients who drive in from Brooklyn to get this done and turn around to go home."

Now that the challenge had been put forward, I said, "Okay. We might as well get it over with."

So Irma and I headed out for a little lunch and even bought some jeans. When we got back, the doctor led me down the hallway to a private procedure room. He explained he would take the sample from my right pelvic bone while I was lying on my stomach. He would give me a local anesthetic to numb everything. The only thing I should feel was pressure and suction from the biopsy needle.

He was absolutely right. I'd probably give it a two out of ten on the pain scale. To be honest, over the course of the next week, it really didn't feel any more uncomfortable than if I had fallen backward onto the sharp corner of a table. It was just like a deep bruise. Now keep in mind, this is just my take on it, but at least a happy ending is possible. After that, I got myself together and went back to Irma.

She asked, "So how was it?"

I answered, "No big deal. Let's go home."

I was told the results would be back in about a week. We made it home. All along the way, I was waiting for the pain to get worse, but it never did.

Things don't automatically get worse just because you have cancer.

About a week passed. I still hadn't heard anything yet, so I called. I was told it would probably be a couple more days.

We finally got the good news. The bone marrow was clear. I was officially declared a "Stage IIA Hodgkin's Lymphoma Patient." The "A" associated with the staging simply signified that I was relatively symptom-free. This referred to symptoms such as night sweats, unexplained weight loss or night pain, and so forth. It seemed as if we had caught it just before things got worse.

I suppose the take-home message would be, if you're not feeling well or even think something's just not right, please go see your doctor.

And if you don't have one, I'll lend you one of mine.

August 11 (Letter to Family and Friends
Regarding Tests {except Bone Marrow})

Hey Gang,

Hope you managed to stay dry today. It was a big day in the city today. I finally met my oncologist at Sloan-Kettering who let us know that the Hodgkin's Lymphoma appears to be isolated to my chest region. This is definitely great news because now they won't have to go fishing around to find it in another part of my body. Having said this I should let you know we're still awaiting the results of the bone marrow biopsy to confirm their assumption about the location. (There still remains a 10% chance or less that some of the active cells are in the marrow but most likely not, due to the results of the other tests)

Treatment is likely to consist of about 4 months of chemo (twice a month) followed by some very localized radiation therapy (about 23 days worth, every day for about a 5 to 10 minute session). Sounds like a lot, I know, but it beats any of the alternatives so keep those prayers comin'.

We're doing well and are very happy with everything so far. Thanks again for your support.

Best Always,

Mark

Chapter Four:

GETTING READY FOR VICTORY

I NOW HAD FIFTEEN days before I would start my chemotherapy. I still needed to get two more simple diagnostic tests done before I started everything: an electrocardiogram (EKG) and an echocardiogram. Both of these were a snap. I had them performed at the hospital where I work.

The EKG was nothing more than a few adhesive electrodes placed at various points on my skin. These electrodes were connected with wires to a machine that measured the activity of my heart. I just had to lay there. It was over in less than a minute. Everything was fine.

The echocardiogram was a little different. An ultrasound wand covered with gel was used to see how healthy my heart looked. The tech placed the wand against my chest and moved it over the area of my heart. The heart looked good. Now I was cleared for chemo.

At a lean one hundred and fifty-seven pounds, I started to wonder what changes, if any, I could expect from the chemotherapy and radiation. I was curious about the physical, mental, emotional and spiritual challenges that might lie ahead. The one thing I knew for certain was I wanted to face everything as the same Mark I had always been.

I even kidded the doctor once by saying, "If these treatments are going to make me any less of a smart-ass than I already am, I might have to reconsider."

He smiled and said, "Don't worry. I think you'll do just fine."

I also felt it would be important to develop some pre-chemo strategies to help keep me in the right mind-set for the treatments. I started **writing a journal** so I could keep a day-by-day record of what I was feeling and doing throughout my treatments. In addition to the journal, I also decided to **take a picture of myself before each treatment** session. Having a visual to go along with the writing would be somewhat cool.

To get a better understanding of what I might experience throughout the whole ordeal, I also **began reading some of the literature** that MSK had given to me, online Web sites, professional journals, and various books.

Many of the books Irma and I went through in the stores were targeted for different cancers other than lymphoma, which was a shame. Many took an approach to coping with cancer that just didn't seem to fit my character and personality so well. Of course, I was able to relate each book's content to my own personal situation; however, I was really hoping to find something exclusive to Hodgkin's with a more proactive approach.

That's part of the reason you're reading these words now.

I also decided to **continue working and exercising**. Maintaining my routine just made more sense to me rather then turning my world upside down while trying to cope with something totally unknown to me. Pulling away from everything that made me, who I was, might possibly put me at a distinct disadvantage in my recovery. In retrospect, modifying my daily patient load and workout intensity was definitely the way for me to go. I also had tremendous support from my co-workers and supervisor, which made these decisions easier. They even gave me and proudly wore violet bracelets in my support that said, "Live Well Laugh Often." Incidentally, as others found out about the bracelets, more were ordered and worn.

Adapting the right mental attitude was another extremely important strategy for me. I remember reading about one person's cancer battle and took note of the point at which she felt she was a cancer survivor. I had never thought about the survivor thing. For me, I just knew **I wanted to be a victor, not a victim**. Lymphoma had waged its war, and it was up to me to defeat it victoriously. I even made some shirts and hats with "Victor Not Victim" and "VNV" on them to wear to my chemo sessions. One doctor thought it was a lot better than the more commonly seen "F#@k Cancer."

Another strategy was to **hold no pity parties** in my honor. Feeling sorry for myself or asking "Why me?" wouldn't help anything. I had to go through this. End of story.

And that's going to be different for each and every person faced with something similar. It doesn't matter how you do it. Just do it! I can tell you, from my own experience, this whole process helped to reaffirm the person I always thought I was. For this, I felt blessed.

Probably one of the strategies that helped me most was my decision to **keep people informed**, firsthand, of everything going on. This meant regular e-mails and phone calls to family, friends, and colleagues. I felt keeping everyone updated was the best way to prevent unnecessary worry and concern. It also turned out to be a great support group, which grew in number over the course of my treatments. My friend, Jen, even used the e-mails as a motivation for her marathon training.

The last major strategy was one I'd stay committed to for the whole ride. I wanted to **play an active role in the decision-making process**. The best way to do that was to trust the medical team laying out the path I needed to follow. I promised to be as open and forthcoming with everything I was doing and feeling. My team, in turn, would help me understand the process and make me aware of all the things I could do to help improve my chances for victory.

I received advice on the importance of keeping up my dietary intake, drinking plenty of fluids, decreasing my sugar intake, avoiding raw foods, avoiding exposure to infection, and even brushing my teeth with fluoride-fortified toothpaste from my dentist. Everyone was on board with the idea of making sure I got through this thing. Now it was up to me. CHARGE!!!

Chapter Five:
MY CHERRY SYRUP

Now THAT I HAD my treatment strategies in place, it was time to get started. I remember that August 31 very clearly. Around six thirty in the morning my in-laws called to wish me well. The night before, I had received the same sort of calls from both my parents and my brother. Irma and I had to be in the city by eleven o'clock. Irma whipped up some French toast and juice. We took my first photo with my first T-shirt, which said,

So I said to the cancer

"My name is VICTOR, NOT VICTIM!"

After that, we got our stuff together and headed to the train station. I have to be honest. There wasn't anything specific going through my mind on the commute in. We got to MSK in plenty of time and just waited to see the doctor. He liked the T-shirt.

A finger-stick blood sample made sure my blood cell count was where it should be. My blood pressure and pulse were measured as well. After the results came back fine, he called the infusion lab to schedule my session.

Irma was able to come along, but we both agreed, only I would be treated that day. What made this particular session unique was it would be the only infusion I'd receive in the city. The rest would be given at the satellite office on Long Island. I was going to receive the ever-popular ABVD chemo cocktail, an acronym for the four main drugs used in treating Hodgkin's lymphoma. The doctor told us it was going to take a couple hours to mix my chemo cocktail, so we were given a beeper and told to come back when beeped.

Irma and I decided to do some window shopping while we waited. At this one store, we got each other something for our upcoming anniversary. We decided it was okay not to surprise each other this year. We went back to the hospital for something to eat. I drank plenty of water that day, so I stayed well hydrated. And while we were sharing a piece of cake, the beeper beeped.

It was time. (If this was an audio book, the suspense music would start now.)

We made our way to the infusion lab. I met my nurse, who briefed me on what was going to happen. She was really sweet, just like everyone else had been. The nurse explained my chemotherapy would be given intravenously (IV) through my forearm. The doctor had already mentioned this to me, so it wasn't a surprise. The other alternative would have involved the placement of a port to the side of my neck, but that wasn't necessary in my case. I never even asked why.

She got me situated in a recliner directly across from a goodie-table filled with wrapped peanut butter and jelly sandwiches, packages of shortbread cookies, and water bottles. I thought, "Maybe this won't be so bad after all."

She gave me an anti-nausea pill to swallow then prepped my left arm for the needle. The needle was so tiny that I barely felt it go in. I had been an avid blood donor for years, and those needles tend to be a little bigger.

Irma hung out right next to me. I did the best I could to keep her pre-occupied by just saying silly things as usual. The first drug delivered through IV was another anti-nausea drug. Everything possible is done so you won't feel sick from the chemo drugs. This IV ran for a half hour.

During that time, Irma and I continued to chat. We even got into conversations with our neighboring patients. No two persons were the same, and neither were their stories. It really was an entirely different experience.

After that first half hour, it was time for the next three drugs (ABV) to be given via IV push. It was explained to me that an infusion nurse would always deliver these drugs in order to ensure my IV line was still flowing. The nurse was able to see this by drawing back on the plunger and looking for my blood in the syringe. If she didn't see my blood, she wasn't allowed to deliver the chemo drug. This helped prevent unnecessary injury to my healthy tissue in the area of the IV.

One of the drugs was as red as the cherry syrup used to make Shirley Temples. Unfortunately, I wasn't being served any of those cocktails today. The delivery of these drugs took another half hour. The fifth IV drug (D) was then hung, and it was delivered over the course of an hour. So, in total, my chemo treatments would last about two hours. All I had to watch out for was sudden fever after each infusion.

At this point, I was allowed to walk around, go to the bathroom, eat, or do just about anything except leave the building. I chose to do a little of each. I even got in a little studying with some anatomical charts I came across during one of my strolls.

Irma kept asking, "So what's it feel like? Do you feel anything different?"

It was like I was expecting to feel the same thing those guys in the movies feel when they change into werewolves. We continued to ask ourselves those same questions after we left the hospital, on the subway, on the train, and even back home, but nothing changed. Aside from feeling a little tired from getting up so early, I felt the same way coming home as I did going in.

We ended up going to McDonald's because we enjoy doing that on Friday nights. Then we came home and hung out. We called our families to let them know how things went, and they asked if I felt any different than usual. I did feel a couple of brief hot flashes, but, then again, I was thirty-seven. Now I just had to keep up with my anti-nausea meds and see how things went.

It was a long weekend because of the holiday. I really just planned to hang out with Irma and Molly. I had made it through the first session, and I only had seven more to go. I was super happy to not feel queasy or uneasy in any way.

After a decent night's sleep, I woke up the next morning with all my parts still attached. I had some eggs with Irma, and I made a couple more calls to family and friends. I started to discover I had been put on worldwide prayer lines by friends of my families, and I even received two handmade prayer blankets that had been put together with a whole lot of love. It was amazing to see how many people were pulling for me. I did my best through phone calls and e-mails to keep them informed.

I started myself on laxatives to help keep regular and maintained my water intake. Except for an increasing fatigue, things were going really well that weekend. At first, we just assumed the fatigue was from the chemo drugs, but we shortly found out that it could be a side effect from my anti-nausea drug. I didn't like that disconnected feeling I was starting to experience. So I looked at the drug label, which read "as needed."

Two days after my first chemo session, I decided to try a day without the anti-nausea medicine. Coming off them made a huge difference and it brought me back to the person I was used to being. I eventually asked for an anti-nausea drug with fewer side effects in case I would need it, but, fortunately, I never did.

Four days after my first chemo infusion, I had an appointment to see the Chief of Medical Oncology at MSK's satellite office on Long Island. He was a great guy, and I was happy to be under his care. I told him I had been feeling fine and hadn't experienced any nausea. I mentioned that I had stopped the anti-nausea meds altogether. That's when I got the other one.

I also found out I wasn't going to have my chemo sessions on Friday, like everybody wants for that extra rest time. Instead, I would go on Mondays. Oh, well. You can't expect everything to go your way now, can you? Hey listen, I was just happy to be getting healthy again, which obviously beat the alternative!

I went back to work five days after the first chemotherapy to a modified schedule of only two patients per hour. On my early days, which was twice a week, I would come in an hour later at eight o'clock and make up the difference using sick time. Another modification was to take off my chemo days with the exception of the second infusion because I already had patients scheduled.

So, I went back to work for the first time after chemo and did pretty well. After work, I went to the gym and did a little cardio/resistance training without any trouble. As I was on my way out, I noticed my reflection in one of the mirrors that lined the gym walls, and had a moment. I thought to myself, "You have cancer, and you don't look any different than anyone else in this place."

I then wondered if there were any other cancer fighters in the room or, even more scary, anyone who had it, but didn't know. It all started with just a cough, remember? The cancer didn't change me unless I let it. That's the cool part that was left up to me. Of course, when my hair started falling out, I changed, but that was only physical. Spiritual, mental, and emotional Mark was going to do way better!

By the end of the first week, I did start to notice a couple things. My fingertips would occasionally lose their sensitivity, but that wasn't so uncommon with this type of chemo. Being a physical therapist, it was slightly concerning to me. I also noticed a little belly cramping even though I was staying regular with my bowel movements at this point. I found limiting heavily seasoned/spicy foods was a little better. And by the middle of the month, I had already put on about three pounds. Everyone except for me was thrilled. Again, it beat the alternative.

On a lighter note, we were getting ready to celebrate our seventh wedding anniversary. Now, most people set aside some special time to be together, and we did, too. But, that weekend, we chose to spend our special day in a classroom with about sixteen other physical therapists. It was something we had planned to do earlier that year, and it just didn't seem we should pass it up just because of my treatments. After all, we had already bought each other something special on my first day of chemo. It's hard to believe that, the next day after our anniversary, and an awesome class, was my second infusion.

Once I finished my morning shift and a co-worker took my picture, I was off to the satellite. Because I had tolerated the first chemo infusion so well, I convinced Irma to let me try the remaining sessions on my own. She was already with me day and night on light sleep mode just in case I needed something. I couldn't even go to the bathroom in the middle of the night without her asking if everything was okay.

Have I mentioned how blessed I am?

After I got there and gave my name, rank, and birth date, I was brought to one of the exam rooms for a finger stick and vitals check. The doctor said the blood counts were a little low, and I would have to start receiving a drug called Neupogen to help bring up my blood cell levels. It was pretty common to go this route, and it would just mean coming to the satellite for an injection during my off-treatment week. As far as the chemo was concerned, I was good to go.

My doctor led me to the infusion lab and a very comfortable recliner, where I met another really wonderful nurse who was ready to hook me up to my juice. She chose the top of my left wrist for the IV needle and started me on fluids.

At the satellite, the drugs were pretty much ready to go. I didn't have to wait for a two-hour prep time. From there on in, it was pretty much the same scenario as the last time. I was given an anti-nausea pill followed by the first half hour bag. Then I had the half hour IV push with the cherry syrup and company. All of this was topped off with an hour supply of Dacarbazine. It was like a six-course meal in two hours, only not as tasty. I still managed to snack, go to the bathroom, and keep myself busy until the time was over. I was then unhooked and free to go home.

On the way home, I gave Irma an update, and once I got in, found her little messages of love for me on the countertop. Molly always managed to greet me at the door in her own special way. I made my calls and sent out my e-mails, which were now starting to grow in recipient size. That made me feel good inside, unlike the constipation that had started about two days later.

In addition to the laxatives, I tried to get the bowels moving one time with a three- mile run, but it didn't help. So, on the fifth day following the chemo, I resorted to using a Fleet enema. I know some of you are thinking "TMI," yet others are thanking me right about now.

Hemorrhoids also started to show their ugly head (no pun intended). An over-the-counter ointment did the trick for me. So I got through the weekend and even managed to co-host a BBQ for friends with a lot less cramping.

On Monday, I had to go back for my first Neupogen injection. After check in, a lovely nurse took me upstairs. She was just as caring a person as all the others.

She asked, "How are things going? Which arm do you prefer?"

I said, "I'm doing well. The left arm will be fine."

I was in and out within ten minutes, so off to work I went.

Work and my time at the gym were going well. It just felt good to keep up with my normal routine. Later, that same week, I did notice a couple of physical changes. My fingernail beds were darkening. I also started experiencing diffuse pelvic and hip pain, making it uncomfortable to sleep and move around. I even resorted to riding a stationary bike at the gym.

The nail beds were another common chemo occurrence that would probably worsen as my treatments went on. The chemotherapy was killing the cancer, but it was also killing any of my other fast-growing tissues. Think about anything that you might have to groom and you can get a better idea of where you might see the most immediate physical changes during chemotherapy.

The soreness in the hips, on the other hand, was just my bone marrow making new cells at an accelerated rate. It actually went away about thirty-six to forty-eight hours after the third Neupogen injection. Again, it was all part of getting better.

Just around that same time, I ran into a colleague whom I hadn't seen for a couple of years. To my surprise, he told me he had been diagnosed with Parkinson's disease, so I told him my good news. We commiserated together. It certainly put things into perspective, reinforcing the fact that we're not invincible or immune to anything that could potentially come our way. Last I heard he was doing well.

As I headed into October, I knew it was going to be a busy month. I was scheduled for three chemo sessions because of the way the days fell. By now, I had developed a strategy for the constipation, including plenty of water, the laxatives, and an over-the-counter powdered laxative that dissolved in my juice. This regime started the day before chemo treatments and finished once the bowels were moving again.

The morning of my third infusion, I took a run to the beach and back. It felt good to still feel like me despite the darkening fingernails and (now) toenails. When I got to the center, it was business as usual. I checked in and waited to be called for my finger stick. Then my doctor gave me the once-over before I was led to the infusion room.

The Neupogen injections had worked well. My levels were well within the safety zone for the chemo drugs. One of the super-nurses greeted me. With one stick to my right wrist, I was off and running... or actually the IV was.

I went home that night feeling pretty much the same as always. I had a minor hot flash here and there, but nothing to really speak of. By the time Irma had gotten home and settled down next to me, it was around nine thirty. She asked if I was feeling well because I looked pale. I had hoped it was just the lighting in the room, but I could see what she meant when I looked in the mirror.

The next day, I woke up with a little more color in my face. I got myself ready for work and headed out. By that afternoon, I was getting warmer and redder in the face. I was told the steroid medications could do this. It did lessen as the day went on and by nighttime, I was fine.

Wednesday came. I headed in to work at eight o'clock. I got more and more tired as the morning went on. By noon, I was starting to feel wiped out, but I still managed to meet Irma for lunch, which helped perk me up enough to finish the day. I did come home and lay down for over an hour. Then I took it easy for the rest of the night.

On Thursday morning, I felt sluggish, but I was better than the day before. Later that morning and by the start of my shift, I seemed to be back to normal. I even made it to the gym after work. I was able to keep up with exercising until the next dose of chemo. This turned out to be a typical pattern that would repeat itself throughout my chemotherapy. My days affectionately became known as: Chemo Monday, Hot Flash Tuesday, Wipeout Wednesday and Transition Thursday.

As October continued to pass by, I was heading in for my fourth chemo session.

Yes, the half-way point.

I was feeling pretty good. I also started becoming increasingly aware of people coughing and sneezing. It sometimes felt like I was surrounded by potential assassins. But people do cough and sneeze, so there wasn't much I could do except stay free from the spray and avoid shaking hands. Keeping a small sample of hand sanitizer in my pocket was also helpful.

The Neupogen was helping to keep my blood levels right where they needed to be. The soreness throughout my pelvis and hips was also lessening, which meant my body was getting used to the injections. My doctor was also sending me for another PET scan to see how things were going. Of course, I thought they were going well, but, then again, I was a little biased.

About that same time, I had finally convinced Irma to visit her parents in the Netherlands for two weeks. It had been quite a while since we had last seen them. I almost had to buy the ticket and force her to go. She didn't like that too much, but we both were able to see how well I was handling everything. Besides, she would only be missing one of the chemo sessions. I ended up taking one of those weeks off, too.

My mother decided to keep me company for a couple of days, while Irma was away. That was nice. She even made it to my fourth infusion.

This was a bigger deal than I realized. My mother got a chance to meet and personally thank my oncologist and everyone else taking care of her baby. Even more importantly, she got to watch her son receive chemotherapy. She realized I really wasn't suffering with my treatments which I felt was a comfort to her.

We went to the movies and ate pizza right after. What could be more convincing than that? It seemed that my mom, my friends, and so many others took greater comfort in seeing that I was doing well as opposed to just hearing that I was doing well.

The trend in fatigue following the chemo stayed the same as before. Prepping my bowels was really helping to keep things more comfortable. I sometimes felt like my own private science experiment, which at least helped me look at things a little more lightheartedly.

So, another week went by. My PET scan appointment finally rolled around. I headed over to a more local imaging center right after my Neupogen injection. I had already prepped the night before with a similar diet. I even remembered to sit down when I went to the bathroom.

As far as the procedure went, it was pretty much the same, but I thought the first barium concoction tasted a little more like a piña colada than this one. Shortly after, I was injected with the radioactive glucose and spent about an hour sliding through the oversized breath mint. After my pictures were taken, I was on my way home. I made my calls, and was happy to hear that Irma was having a good visit with her family.

The call I got the next morning was one that I'll never forget. My oncologist called to tell me the cancer was just about gone. His words were almost as sweet as Irma's "I do." The chemo was working and so was I.

After hanging up the phone, I thanked God for enabling me to heal and continue enjoying all his gifts I was given to enjoy. I was so happy to call Irma and share the good news with her. I could hear the sigh of relief in her voice after which, she told me she loved me. We were both so happy that it was going in the direction we always hoped it would.

The physical changes were really kicking in now. Losing my body hair and darkening nails was a regular thing, but I knew those were only temporary. The mental, spiritual and emotional attitudes were far more important to keep in check. Fortunately, they were! I did, however, notice I was more emotionally vulnerable to sad or heartfelt occurrences. For example, a tragic news story that might normally only catch my interest would make me fill up and want to cry. Chick flicks were almost guaranteed to start the tears flowing, especially those with a cancer theme. Perhaps I was getting through this with some suppressed emotions, but I thought the trade-off was worth it.

The PET scan was essentially negative after all.

As October came to a close, I'd be heading in for my fifth infusion. I was happy that Irma was back. It was great to finally have her home and, more specifically, in my arms. We had a lot to celebrate and be thankful for.

The fifth chemo session was a little uncomfortable with three sticks because my veins weren't fully cooperating. This isn't so uncommon with IV treatments. I also noticed my forearm feeling somewhat cold during the infusions. Even though the drugs were at room temperature, it just felt cold. This was, again, not so uncommon. From then on, I just wore a sweatshirt that I could rest over the infusion site to keep it warm. I also wore sweatpants that could easily drop when I went to the bathroom during treatments. It just was one less thing I had to fuss with.

By the time November rolled around I was already more than halfway done with my chemo. Due to indigestion, antacids, especially berry-flavored, were becoming a regular part of my diet. My diet was leaning more toward food with sweeter or tangier flavors mainly because of my loss of taste. Water even lost its taste. Again, some of you readers know exactly what I'm talking about. This was fortunately only most prevalent during infusion weeks.

I also had a couple nights of sweating and itchy skin which got me concerned. After all, these were some of the things I had felt when this all began. It was important that I stayed focused. I realized that these things can and will happen for reasons other than cancer. Just remember to keep your head screwed on tight...but not too tight!

With the fall also came the burden of picking up the pretty leaves. Feeling a little less energetic, Irma and I just worked together at an easy pace and managed to get everything done. Thank God for Irma and the leaf blower.

Have I at all mentioned how blessed I am to have her?

I tried to stay active and keep up with the gym. It seemed exercising helped me to maintain my focus. My sleep was important, too. Missing a regular night's sleep could easily impact the next day, but fortunately, those were few and far between.

By the time of my sixth infusion, I was still getting good grades on my report card. Blood levels were staying where they were supposed to, making it easier to keep a regular routine. I had been drinking tons of water to hopefully make it through with one stick, and it seemed to work.

My only problem happened after treatment. I had forgotten to wear sweatpants that day. Because I was so full from the infusion (plus what I drank), I had to take a pee rather badly.

Once the nurse removed my IV and bandaged my arm, I ran to the bathroom, but, because my jeans wouldn't cooperate, my puncture site started bleeding from the extra force needed to quickly lower my jeans. After mission accomplished, I got another gauze wrap to match my new black and blue. The next time, I made sure to remember my sweatpants and take a pee before the last drug bag was empty. With two more infusions to go, I thought I could handle at least that much.

More physical changes were occurring. My eyelashes had fallen out, making sunny days a bit sunnier for me. I never really gave them that much thought before. My nails were really dark by now. In fact, when I would see a patient for the first time, I'd usually just say that I wasn't too handy with a hammer. I let some of them in on the secret, but many never paid it much attention. My eyebrows were also starting to go. I can honestly say this was the one physical change that did bother me.

I never realized how important they were for facial expressions. It was a little bit of a bummer, but I managed. My overall endurance was also starting to become a factor. On a scale from zero to ten (with ten being my normal), I would sometimes feel as low as a six or seven. My concentration seemed to also be slightly affected, and multitasking took a bit more effort.

Irma would also have to occasionally remind me of get-togethers with friends along with other engagements. It wasn't that those things weren't important. Rather, they just never seemed to stick in my head like before. Some literature affectionately referred to it as *chemobrain* or *chemofog*. Even though this would become more prevalent later, I still had to keep trudging through day by day while getting things done. I also felt the exercise was helping with that as well.

Another physical change I noticed was that my veins seemed to be firming up where I was receiving the infusions. The chemo drugs were beating them up a little. I was happy to learn that over time they'd take care of themselves.

I finally made it to Thanksgiving. Believe me, this year more than ever, we were all very thankful for the way things were going. I was happy to hit this milestone. Having dinner with my family at my brother and sister-in-law's was great even though I was ready to lay down at four o'clock for a little rest. I guess it was to save energy for the Christmas shopping we'd be doing the next day.

A couple days later, I was in for my seventh chemo session. I was still getting the Neupogen and my levels were staying where they needed to be. The only major difference that day was that I hadn't kept up with my water intake. To this day, I blame that for the reason it took seven sticks to complete my infusion.

Yes, I said seven sticks. Ouch!

For the first couple, it seemed my veins were a little too firm. The next couple, my blood wasn't back-flowing well enough to allow the IV push. Everyone felt horribly. Each of the nurses wants everything to go off without a hitch. The more sticks there are, the worse they feel. I'll always be grateful for all their help in getting me healthy again, but I can honestly say that I was happy when that session was over. On the way home I stopped to visit a couple friends who were glad to see me plugging along.

Now that it was December, I felt the year truly coming to a close. That month, I would have my last chemotherapy session, take my final physical therapy course for the year, and, even more importantly, make it to Christmas 2007.

When I was driving along one day, it started snowing. I thought to myself how the snow just seemed magical in some way. I always enjoyed the first snowfall. My strength and endurance were even more affected by now, so I would just ask for help when I needed it. There were no points for a defeatist attitude.

About that same time, our septic tanks seemed to be getting full so I called for service. I went outside ahead of time to dig up our caps, and I got winded really easily. Through the window, Irma could clearly see that her hubby was changing, but she supported my effort and allowed me to pace myself to get the job done. Everything worked out fine.

My gym sessions were now mainly consisting of treadmill walking and stretching. I was more focused on trying to prevent any further decline in my conditioning.

Finally, on December 10, my last chemo session arrived. I drank plenty of fluids in preparation, which seemed to pay off because I only needed one stick throughout the whole session.

I brought a big basket of chocolate truffles for the staff at MSK to thank them for everything they had done for me over the last four months. Later that evening, I attended the first day of a three-day mission at our church, which turned out to be a bit of a challenge because I was kind of pooped.

A Franciscan friar was running the mission, and he kept things pretty lively with some good jokes, which even helped get me through my Wipeout Wednesday.

The next day, however, was a true blessing. I woke up to a small snowstorm, which meant I didn't have to go to work and got an extra day of rest. Apparently, attending the mission paid off in more ways than one. The rest of the week was a snap.

That same weekend, the hospital was hosting a class I was supposed to teach, but I didn't, because of everything going on. I stopped by with doughnuts to say hello and let everyone know I was doing fine. Again, it seemed good for them to see me almost as much as it was nice for me to see them.

Now away from the chemo and Neupogen, I noticed I wasn't dragging so much. Each day, I felt a little better and decided to set a new goal for myself. I wanted to be jogging three miles before starting my radiation therapy, and I did it.

I used the treadmill for interval training, switching off with walking and running until I eventually got up to three miles in just over a half hour. The whiskers were starting to grow back on my face, but I still didn't have my eyebrows. I was also starting to have regular bowel movements with less need for the antacids.

The best gifts I opened on Christmas 2007 were my own eyes.

Think about that for a moment.

Just six months ago, when my cancer had been found, I was crying wondering if I was going to make it to Christmas. Well, I had made it. Even though I still had the radiation to face, I knew that things would be all right.

55

September 1 (1 Down and 7 to Go)

Good Morning All,

Figured I'd just bring you up to speed with the cancer thing. I went for my first chemo treatment yesterday. The actual drug delivery time was 2 hours but you can either sit or walk around or even sneak a little sandwich when you want so it goes by kinda fast. The nurses were very accommodating and the other patients were just as nice and supportive to each other. So far, no ill effects except for a couple of hot flashes last night but I had a good night's sleep and plan to take it easy for the weekend. They gave me anti-nausea meds and I'll probably take them at least 'til Monday and then see.

I want to just thank you all again for your tremendous support, thoughts and prayers. My staff really surprised me at work by going to www.wristbands-with-a-message.com to buy colored wrist bands for Hodgkin's Disease (a nice color purple if I do say so myself). Their choice message was "Live Well Laugh Often". I saw them feverishly pull out their wrist bands and put them on. They said they couldn't wait to do it for me. Well, I could have cried.

I'm hoping and praying for smooth sailing but especially for my white blood cells to stay high so the chemo can continue uninterrupted. For now, I'm going to have a little French toast for breakfast.

Enjoy the day. I know I will.

Love,

Mark

September 18 (Chemo Round 2)

Dear Friends and Family,

Yesterday was treatment #2 at the Sloan-Kettering satellite clinic. Everything went very well. My blood count was good except for one white blood cell count so they will give me an extra few injections of medicine to boost it up. This is rather typical in a case like mine. Please, no worries.

I had a rather large breakfast this morning of a roll and 4 egg whites with juice. Believe me, I'm very thankful that the nausea thing hasn't been a factor. Let's continue to hope and pray that that will be the case throughout. Now that bikini season is over, I'll keep warmer with a few extra pounds.

Keep your thoughts and prayers coming. I thank you dearly for them.

Peace, Love and Happiness

Mark

October 2 (Chemo 3 and Feelin' Symptom Free)

Hey Everyone,

I just wanted to let you know that #3 went well leaving only 5 more treatments to go. Next visit will make it half-way over. So far, so good. My doctor wants to get a PET scan done after #4 to see if "The Juice" he's got me on is working (studies say if the PET scan shows good things, then good things are what we can continue to expect).

Irma and I also wanted to thank you for your ongoing prayers and support. It's great to know how our family circle keeps growing larger and stronger.

All our best to you (and you, and you and you and you and you -Sorry, just watched The Sound of Music)

Mark

October 16 (4 Down. 1/2-Way There)

Hey Everyone,

I just wanted to update you after chemo treatment #4. I've managed to keep a regular energy level all day but expect a little sluggishness through Thursday. By Thursday night it's generally back to a light gym night.

I do very much appreciate all your continued support and prayers and just need you to know how tremendously encouraging and motivational they are. Coming up this Monday I have the pleasure of another PET scan to see how things are going. A little scary but I must say that same overwhelming peace and comfort I've felt throughout, leads me to believe things are moving in the right direction. These pictures will definitely be worth more than a thousand words. That might just match the bill amount. Thank God for the health insurance and all the other wonderful things we're blessed with! Irma and I both send our thanks.

Warm regards on a chilly night,

Mark

October 29 (5th Chemo Treatment Done and Over With)

Hey Gang,

I hope this message finds you well. #5 went off without a hitch. The doctor is happy with everything and oh, by the way, my PET scan was negative (did someone just say my PET scan was negative because I'm pretty sure someone just said that my PET scan was negative). Of course this means there is NO cancer activity. Celebration is surely in order. You can't imagine how happy I am to be sending the good news and believe me, I know it wouldn't be possible without your prayers and support. Thank you! I am forever grateful and promise to keep up things on my end.

Irma and I are enjoying the good news and doing well. I look forward to the last 3 treatments and starting the radiation therapy. The research shows that the combination of treatments work best to fully eradicate the cancer. I feel things will continue to go well. Please keep the positive vibes comin'.

Thanks again for all your support,

Mark

November 13 (Chemo #6 and Heading Down the Home Stretch)

Good Evening Everyone,

Well, 6 down and 2 to go. Quite frankly it's getting a little old. I swear I can taste 1 of the drugs on any given day while I'm driving around. Chances are, NOT, but it does spoil my in-car singing performances from time to time. (Pearl Jam and Dylan, especially) It hasn't affected my air guitar riffs. (Thank God) Everything else seems to be going well. I do have a little less energy every now and then so I try to make sure I'm keeping up with my sleep. Getting to the gym also helps but most of all, everyone's thoughts and prayers. I'm certain I'm much healthier for it. Again, we thank you for everything you do to help this process along. For now I'll continue my closet performances and maybe someday in a karaoke bar, I can make you laugh as a token of my appreciation. (Some of you have already had this experience and lived to tell)

Much Love and Stay Well,

Mark

November 27 (7 Down 1 to Go)

Hello Everyone,

I hope you had a great Thanksgiving. There was certainly no shortage of things to be thankful for this year.

Today was a mixed day. All my blood levels are where they should be and together with the remission earns me a gold star for the day. The treatment session was quite a different story. Today I felt like a Haitian Voodoo Doll. 7 sticks to get all the drugs in just because my veins didn't want to play nice with the nurses. You'd think after watching American Gangster I would have at least learned how to make my veins more accessible to others. Still, all things considered, ONLY 1 MORE CHEMO SESSION!!

What next you ask? Radiation therapy, of course. I contacted the department and let them know I'd like to start ASAP to which they told me there's a process to follow and I'd be contacted within a few days or so. {otherwise, control freak might come out to play (YIKES!)}

I always thank you for your continued support, prayer and encouragement and this e-mail is no different. Thank you for all your support, prayer and encouragement. It really means a ton.

Peace, Love and Happiness,

Mark, Irma and Molly, the dog

December 11 (Chemo Phase Over, Radiation Phase On-Deck)

Hello Everyone,

Chemo session 8 of 8 went-off without a hitch. It could be summed up as follows:

Holiday Chocolate for Care Givers:	*$60*
Co-payment for Normal Blood Levels/ 1 Needle Stick	*$20*
Sharing Christmas 2007 with Family and Friends	*Priceless*

Thank you for all your e-mails, laughter, support and prayers. Radiation will start the 9th of January. You can count on the return of my updates. I hope to see most of you over the holidays but if not, Merry Christmas and Happy New Year. Enjoy every minute of time as a precious gift. Time truly is.

Much peace, love and happiness,

Mark

Chapter Six:

PHASE TWO

WELL, I FINALLY MADE it through the chemo and the year was ending. It was great to have made it to Christmas, but it was even better to know how well I was doing.

The radiation was going to begin. I affectionately named it "Phase Two of Get Mark Healthy." Now, before the treatments started, I had to meet with the radiation oncologist and go through two processes referred to as the radiation mapping and simulation. The day of my mapping was New Year's Eve.

Sort of symbolic don't you think?

When I got to the satellite, I met two of the radiation technicians who would help make up the team responsible for my care. Again, just like everyone else, they were great. I was led to a room where I was given a robe in exchange for my shirt. They brought me into another much larger room where my mapping would be performed.

Incidentally, it was the same room where my radiation therapy would take place. This "bunker," as it was referred to, was entirely lined with leaded walls to make sure no radiation leaked out during treatments. To one side was the control room where the technicians could safely oversee things and still avoid exposure. In the middle of the room was a platform table in line with a huge machine, called a linear accelerator. It was responsible for delivering my radiation. And no, it didn't look like a big laser gun or anything like that.

Coming off that machine were two large arms, which actually reminded me of really big headphones from the 1970s. The table could be adjusted to fit each patient right between them.

A picture was then taken of me so I could visually identify myself before each treatment, along with last name spelling and birth date. My radiation oncologist came in just as we finished the photo shoot. I had the pleasure of meeting her back in August to go over a little of what I could expect throughout my radiation treatments. She was very pleased with my progress and expected me to do just fine. She also reviewed some of the things I should be aware of throughout the radiation, like skin dryness, reddening in the treatment area, and a potential sore and scratchy throat. All of which would be temporary and easily managed with a skin moisturizer and a softer diet as needed.

We also went over the mapping process and its importance. Part of the mapping process required me to be fitted for my own personal mold. This mold was made with the use of chemicals that were mixed together and then spread evenly within a large plastic bag. I was then asked to lay with my back on the bag filled with this pasty mixture. I was told not to move. Within a few minutes, the chemicals reacted with each other and started to rise and harden, creating a rigid, foam casting of my upper body. The foam never rose above the front of the body, so there was no need for concern. This was a unique situation for me because I now actually had a mold of myself, which meant maybe more of me could be made. Personally, it's probably safer for everyone that never happens.

Once the mold was created, it was then placed on the platform table. I was asked to lay in it. Now it was time for my tattoos. They raised the table, and it brought me into a position where my body was lined up with small beams of light coming out from the walls and overhead. These light beams were used to locate points on my body and help line me up for the radiation therapy. Once I was in place, the tech used a small needle with ink to permanently tattoo me so these points could always be used during the positioning process. I got seven in total.

It was just another safety mechanism, like the Marky mold, to ensure the radiation was delivered precisely to the exact same location. Of course, my radiation oncologist and a physicist determined each measurement and dosage of treatments. No margin of error would be acceptable to this team. I was really happy about that, and it's something you should take comfort in. After all that, I was free to go.

Well, sort of.

I had a follow-up chest CAT scan scheduled one hour later, but that would be a snap. It was just much of the same breathing in and out while I was slid through the big breath mint. Once that was done, I headed home to help Irma get things ready our big New Year's Eve bash.

Me, her, and the dog.

I just about made it to midnight. Believe me. I knew 2008 was going to be a lot better than 2007.

About a week later, I went back to MSK for my radiation simulation. This was the dry run set up just one day before the first radiation treatment. I changed into another robe, and another tech on the team led me into the bunker. Once inside, I met the fourth and final tech who'd be getting me through these next seventeen sessions.

I was staring down the pike at seventeen radiation sessions Monday through Friday for the next three-and-a-half weeks. Because of the frequency, I decided to readjust my work schedule and take off Wednesdays and Fridays, but I kept my meetings on Tuesdays. I would also have a follow-up appointment with my radiation oncologist every week and a chest x-ray every two weeks. The coolest part was that I'd finish on January 31. I had hoped I'd be done before February, and it looked like that would be the case.

Feeling more and more like me was also a definite plus. Being up to three miles of jogging by now was even more a plus

So, I was in the bunker. I was asked if the guy in the scary photo on the screen was me. Reluctantly, I said yes, along with spelling my last name and saying my birth date. I would have to repeat that same sequence seventeen more times. The Marky mold, all warm and toasty, was up on the platform table, just waiting for me. Once I got on the table and into the mold, everyone huddled around me, making sure I was all lined up.

They used the tattoo markings to line me up with the light beams as the table was raised, positioning me under one of the arms of the radiation machine. This was just a simulation so all the final details of positioning, isolation of the radiation field, and instructions for me were reviewed with a fine-toothed comb. After all that, I was free to go.

Incidentally, the radiation was very small and extremely limited to the field of treatment which contained my neck down to my mid-chest line. There was no concern I'd start glowing or turn into a human flashlight. It just doesn't work like that.

January 9 finally came. I was off to my first radiation treatment. Of course, almost similar to the first chemo day, I was thinking about what it would feel like and what immediate changes I might experience. It was really nice that Irma was able to come along. She had been taking off Wednesdays in addition to her usual Fridays since this ordeal had begun.

Have I told you how blessed I am to be her husband?

Just before I went to the changing room to get my robe I gave Irma a kiss and said, "I hope it's not too long."

I got in my robe. One of my team members escorted me into the bunker. Again, I was asked to identify the photo (yikes!), my last name, and birth date. I got onto the table and laid down in the mold. I was then placed into position. The table was resting between the two arms of the machine. With one arm over me and one under me, I was ready for takeoff.

I was staring up at the big arm overhead. I only saw a little light shining down on me, outlining the treatment field. The techs left the room and said they'd be right back. The only thing I heard after the door closed was a high-pitched buzz for about seventeen seconds. Two of the techs came back in to readjust one of the machine's settings. Then they pushed a button, which caused the two arms to rotate and switch positions.

They said they'd be right back and left the room. I heard that seventeen-second buzzing again. Everyone came back into the room when the buzzing stopped and said I was finished. Believe me. I was just as surprised as you probably are.

I asked, "Is this what I could expect each time?"

The techs said, "Most likely."

I went back to the dressing room to change and put some moisturizer over the treatment area. When I went back to the waiting room, Irma was surprised to see me.

She asked, "When do you go in?"

I said, "I'm already done."

She was shocked. We headed home and noticed no wolf man side effects so, of course, it was e-mail time.

The following visits would continue to be a repeat of everything I just described.

By the time of the fifth visit, I started to see a return of my eyebrows. Thank God! It had already been about a month from the last chemo, and I was just about a third of the way through my radiation therapy. I also noticed a slight darkening of my skin within the treatment field. It sort of looked like I was tanning in January. I had been seeing my radiation oncologist regularly throughout the treatments, and she was pleased with everything. I was even jogging more regularly at the gym.

The eighth treatment was business as usual, but it was also Irma's birthday. I surprised her with tickets for a Broadway show she had wanted to see. We even got to go backstage with one of the actors, courtesy of a close, mutual friend.

It was an awesome evening, but I couldn't help but notice a little soreness in my throat. The soreness started to get worse, and I noticed it most when swallowing crunchy or firm foods. Soft foods were much easier and drinking fluids was even better.

It was obvious the radiation was irritating my throat, but this was only for a short time, and it cleared up within a week after my last treatment. The radiation oncologist was always willing to give me something for the soreness, but I found just switching to softer foods like oatmeal, pasta, and an occasional nutrition shake would do the trick. Let's not forget the healing effects of ice cream either!

My follow-up x-ray went well on the tenth treatment. By the fifteenth, I was sporting a tan similar to summertime Mark. I hadn't tanned in quite some time, and it was likely to stay that way.

I also noticed a return of all body hair. It was like hitting puberty all over again.

Jogging on the treadmill was getting easier. I was even up to two three-mile runs a week. Then the moment I had been waiting for finally came on January 31, 2007.

I received my last cancer treatment.

I brought in another basket of chocolate truffles as a small token of my appreciation. The team gave me a small diploma congratulating me. I even got to take the Marky-mold home.

They were so sweet and always treated me with the utmost kindness. After a whole bunch of hugs and handshakes, I said good-bye and headed to my car for the performance of a lifetime. I think I sang along as loud as I could for about forty-five minutes until I got to work. If the police had pulled me over for speeding, I think I might have gotten out of my car and danced with the officer. I felt invincible, even though I knew I wasn't.

Irma and I celebrated that night with a little sparkling wine and a toast to good health. She also gave me a beautiful card telling me how much she loved me. With all we had been through together, we were able to finally close that chapter in our lives.

Or at least we thought so.

January 10 (Let the Radiation Begin!)

Hello Good People,

I hope the New Year is treating you well. Irma and I really enjoyed the holidays and were happy to see some of you along the way.

Phase 2 of "Get Mark Healthy" began this past Wednesday. Now having had the second dose of radiation I can only hope it continues to go this easily. The treatment sessions are extremely brief (literally about 17 seconds for my back and also for my chest) and the area that is radiated is about the size of a grapefruit. The part that takes the most time is driving to the facility and getting into position. I lay with my upper body in a custom foam mold so I'm always in the same position. The techs then fine-tune the positioning where I stay until it's over. By the way, the table is standing between the 2 giant arms of the Linear Accelerator (or what I like to call the "Laser Gun"). When you hear the beep, you're getting treated (mind you, everyone has cleared the room and are hiding behind some very thick walls and an expensive door for their own protection). The treatment time/dosage may vary from session to session but there are no unpleasantries experienced. Later into the treatments I may develop a sore throat or a dry cough but nothing so far.

I'm back to the endurance training which seemed to slack during the holidays. Earlier I ran about a half hour on the treadmill. It feels good to feel strong again. Thanks for being a part of the strengthening process.

Love,

Mark

January 23 (More Than 1/2-Way With Only 6 to Go)

Hey Everyone,

I hope this e-mail finds you well. I just wanted to let you know that everything is going well. The radiation treatments haven't changed since my last e-mail. They still remain the equivalent of a drive-thru at your favorite fast food joint (no longer than 30 seconds in total). As far as the side-effects go, I've started with a sore throat mainly with swallowing (hold the jokes, please). The radiated skin area feels like a slight sunburn only when scratched or when I'm drying myself off. Overall, pretty easy to deal with but I'll be happy next Thursday when everything comes to an end. Stay tuned!!!!!!!!

Peace, Love and Happiness,

Mark

February 1 (Can You Hear the Fat Lady
Singing, 'Cause It's Over)

Greetings Friends,

As the little subject box says "It's over". I had my last blast of radiation yesterday. The doctor is very pleased with the way things have gone almost as much as Irma and I are. Of course when people ask me what will I do now I can't help but answer "I'm going to Disney World" (but not really). Irma and I do have a get away plan (with much sun screen) but we're also considering a unique continuing education opportunity (I'm pretty sure the fun-in-the-sun thing is going to win out).

On a slightly more serious note, I'd like to try and express my gratitude for all your help. While reading the e-mails sent over the last several months I noticed a few things. The first message announcing my health concerns made it to about 8 people and now this one makes it to over 45. All your responses made me smile more than my mailings made you laugh (I hope). Perhaps most of all, it was very clear that my concerns became your concerns and as we all prayed for the best outcome, I just wanted you to know that I prayed in thanksgiving for each and every one of you. I have been truly blessed to be writing this message to you, but even more so, for being allowed to share a life so very much worth living with so many beautiful and loving people.

Thank you dearly and now please remove your wristbands (especially you Mr. Timms)

Much peace, love and happiness to you,

Mark

Chapter Seven:
THE FOG FINALLY LIFTED

OKAY! SO THE TREATMENTS are over. There is no more cancer. Mark is on the mend, and there are no more problems, right? Well, that lasted for about five days. Don't worry. It wasn't the return of my cancer, so just keep reading.

Remember how I said I had been running rather steadily throughout the radiation? This is something the overachievers should take note of. Feeling as well as I did with everything now behind, I figured I'd add another three-mile run to keep the progression going. Boy, was that a mistake! The problem was that I wouldn't find out until the next day.

On Sunday morning, I took a run on a treadmill and kept my pace pretty steady between six and six-and-a-half miles per hour. I finished up strong and really didn't think much of it aside from being so happy that I could.

Monday marked my official return to work now that I was free and clear of any problems. Around one fifteen that afternoon, I began to feel some discomfort in the front of my neck. I thought I might have slept weird or something, but the discomfort gradually started getting worse as the day went on. It seemed to intensify as I became more active and got better when I stopped moving. I had a steady schedule of patients and managed to get through the evening. At times, I would have to briefly walk away from what I was doing just to catch my breath. By the evening the discomfort had become an intense pain, at least eight out of ten on the infamous pain scale.

I was really starting to freak out my co-workers. Even though I wasn't feeling so hot, I still didn't think it was anything life-threatening. I had no pain radiating into my arm or shoulder region. It was only in my neck. The pain seemed to present itself like an inflammatory process of some sort. Having just finished the radiation, I thought maybe my tissue was more irritated than I realized. The only thing that didn't make sense to me was that, when I tried to lie down, the pain immediately increased, and it became really hard to breathe.

Most of you reading this would already have been on their way to the hospital by now, but remember in the early part of this book when I mentioned a couple of bad decisions that I had made? This was the other one!

I was very happy to leave work that evening. I just tried to remain as relaxed as I could. Even making turns while driving caused the pain to intensify. I made it home and noticed walking a slow shuffle was better than my regular stride. Going upstairs was even more of a challenge. One step at a time with about a five-second rest on each step was the best I could do.

I tried to lie down again, but that was a definite no-go. Sitting down on the soft chair in our bedroom with my feet up and doing nothing but breathing worked just fine for me. This is exactly the way Irma found me. To put it mildly, she was a bit concerned. I explained the whole situation to her and exactly how I was feeling. I somehow convinced her that I wanted to see how I was doing in the morning before I went to the doctor. I thought maybe the pain would go away just as it came on, but I would definitely contact my doctor either way. I also mentioned to Irma that I'd sleep downstairs so I wouldn't keep her from sleeping. I said I'd take the phone with me in case I had to call for an ambulance.

Once she stopped looking at me as if I had four heads and blue skin, she said, "If you think for one second that I'm…" The rest was said out of love and concern.

I slept upstairs that night. I managed at least four or five hours of sleep reclined in the chair. When I first got up, it wasn't too bad, but the pain started to creep up on me again within a half hour. I then made two phone calls: one to work to let them know I wasn't coming in that day and one to MSK. Of course, at that time, I reached the service and waited for a call back.

I thought contacting MSK first was the best bet rather than going to the emergency department. All along, I had that feeling it was some kind of inflammatory process. With consideration of the radiation, I thought MSK should be my first medical contact. A little while had gone by before I got a return call.

After I explained what was going on, I was told to come in. Irma had already let her work know she wouldn't be in and off to the satellite we went. To top things off, it was a cold and very rainy day.

The drive took about forty minutes but seemed like forever. All I could do was try to make myself comfortable. I felt every bump and crack in the road that day. When we got to MSK, Irma dropped me off and went to park the car. As I shuffled in, halfway slumped over, every single employee who had ever seen me before did a double take. With this being far from my normal grand entrance, everyone knew something wasn't quite right with me. Irma came in just after I checked into the radiation oncology department.

After sitting for about five minutes, I made my way over to the reception area and softly said to a really friendly guy I came to know, "I gotta see someone now. This ain't good."

Immediately, he called a nurse. In I went with the help of a wheelchair. Irma was right by my side. Once we were in the room, I explained everything in detail to her and my radiation oncologist, who came in almost immediately after. Both were concerned, given how well I had always presented and even more so because they were having trouble finding the pulse in my right wrist. I was then wheeled across the hall to the medical triage department where a wonderful nurse practitioner and another doctor examined me.

An EKG was performed which came back pretty normal. Because everyone there had done everything she or he could do for me, it was decided I would be transferred to the local hospital for further testing and examination. As good fortune would have it, that particular hospital was also part of the same Catholic Health Services I work for. Again, those hidden blessings always seemed to pop up when I needed them most.

I was going to be transported by ambulance, which meant Irma was going to have to follow behind. The police and EMTs were super nice and made sure Irma knew where she was going. I gave her a kiss before I was loaded into the ambulance.

As we drove away, I saw Irma following behind, but she was starting to fade into the dreary and rainy distance through the small windows on the back of the ambulance. I never felt as alone as I did at that moment.

As we made our way toward the hospital, the crew called in to the emergency department. It was decided to start treating me with a similar protocol used for heart attack patients. Even though I wasn't having a heart attack, aspirins were given to me as a precautionary measure. I was greeted in the ambulance bay by a lovely team of medical professionals, who were very serious about getting me better.

I had another EKG, which again came back normal. Then I had some blood taken. By this time, Irma finally arrived. I was so happy to see her. What was funny was that she had felt that same loneliness just about the very moment we lost sight of each other on the road.

The attending doctor ordered a chest x-ray, an echocardiogram, and a CAT scan of the chest with contrast, which meant I needed an IV. I wasn't too keen on getting stuck after everything I had been through over the last couple months, but I knew it had to be done. I asked the nurse if she could at least try for a larger vein, even if it meant I would have to keep from moving my arm. Thankfully, she agreed. It still didn't feel too great, but at least it only took one try. I even saw Irma wince.

The hospital was busy, so things moved a little slowly. Everyone kept checking in on me to make sure I was okay. In the time I was there, I overheard my oncologist call twice. It felt good inside to feel that cared for. The results of the x-ray and chest CAT scan were normal. The echocardiogram finally showed what was going on. There was a small accumulation of fluid around my heart causing all the fuss.

Surrounding everyone's heart is a small, thin sac called the pericardium. It contains a little fluid that helps to protect and cushion the heart. This sac can sometimes become irritated and inflamed causing pain and swelling to occur.

What was finally deduced was that the crazy amount of running I was doing, in combination with the radiation therapy ended up being just too much for my little body. I would have been fine with the radiation if I had just cut back on my running. All I needed to do was take a little vacation from exercise for a while and perhaps be a little less goal-oriented.

Regular day-to-day stuff at work or low-grade activities was fine, but I was told to avoid anything intensive or strenuous for about two months. I was also given a prescription for Prednisone to help with the inflammation. Within four days, I was able lie down again without any pain or shortness of breath.

It wasn't long after putting my running on hold that I started to notice a change in my ability to concentrate. I was having trouble focusing on things, especially to detail. My mind felt sort of hazy or in a fog. Occasionally I would lose track of what I was saying. Sometimes I had to stop in mid-sentence and search for the word. It just didn't seem to be as smooth a delivery as I was accustomed to.

A while back, a friend had mentioned a phenomenon that some called *chemobrain* or *chemofog*. It seemed that some individuals who had undergone chemotherapy reported experiencing difficulty with memory, multitasking, learning, and processing speed. Some literature suggests this is prevalent in 20 to 30 percent of chemo patients.

What I found even more interesting was that some of the suggested ways to help combat it involved keeping a journal, maintaining a routine, talking about your concerns, and exercise, especially aerobic exercise.

The entire time I had been treated, I kept a journal, maintained a routine, kept an open line of communication with others, and exercised. Now that I wasn't able to exercise, I thought it was oddly coincidental that I was starting to notice these changes.

I know Irma would remind me of things every now and then, but it just seemed to be more obvious to me at this point.

I was mainly concerned because I was scheduled to co-teach a four-day seminar with a good friend of mine to about twenty physical therapists in April. The preparations alone took a lot of focus but, fortunately, it was material I used on a daily basis. The course went well, and I owe a big thanks to my buddy Ed for getting me through it. I had a few momentary lapses in reason, but I covered them up with a sip from the water bottle.

Remember, you should always have a strategy!

It was nice to read the course evaluations afterward to see how much everyone enjoyed our lectures and demonstrations. Nobody seemed to notice a thing. I felt like this was a good exercise in helping me get back on track.

Speaking of exercise, I was cleared about a week later to do anything I wanted, but, I decided to take it a little slower this time.

As the days and weeks passed, I was really doing well. I kept having good follow-up visits with my doctors. I was on a steady return to work and exercise.

In late April, I took my dad to Washington DC for his seventieth birthday. It was nice to show him around and just spend some good quality time together. I know it meant a lot to him, and it certainly did for me.

A few weeks later, Irma and I went to Arizona for almost two weeks. It was the first long vacation we had taken by ourselves in six years. We drove all over the state, hitting places like Phoenix, Sedona, the Navajo Nation, and the Grand Canyon. On some days, we'd hike for as long as six hours, and I never felt tired. It was absolutely beautiful and very humbling with views that would take your breath away.

Shortly after our return from Arizona, I was off to New Hampshire to meet my old college buddies. Every year, they camp and usually hike Mt. Washington. I wasn't always able to make the trips, but this year, I was in.

It was good to see everyone doing so well. They were also happy to see that things were going well for me. It was a tough climb, but it felt super good to make it to the peak. I even bought a sweatshirt and posed for a picture with my "Victor Not Victim" hat to help mark the accomplishment.

My in-laws came to visit later that summer for three-weeks. They hadn't seen me for quite some time and were happy I was doing well. E-mails and photos are one thing, but, they can never replace time spent with those you love. We even managed to sneak in a mini-vacation through New England with them. It was great having them, but, as always, it was hard to see them go. The best thing is that, now that I'm not on illness alert, we can go and visit them anytime we want.

This past year was filled with a lot of trials and obstacles. Some were a little easier to overcome than others, but the main point is that, with the right physical, mental, emotional, and spiritual mind-set, I was able to make it through everything.

My one piece of advice to anyone going through something similar would be to play an active role in your own health care. Don't be afraid to ask for help when you need it. I believe the world is full of wonderful people who can oftentimes do more for you than you could ever imagine. I know this because I am blessed to be surrounded by these very people, whom I will never be able to fully express how much their strength and support has really meant to me. I only hope that, after reading this, I've been able to help you the same way they helped me. If anything is still unclear, call me!

Peace, Love, and Happiness, Mark.

Breinigsville, PA USA
29 September 2009
224884BV00001B/2/P

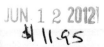